KEEPERS OF THE WILD

A TRUE STORY TOLD THROUGH THE EYES OF THE ANIMALS
SECOND EDITION

By DOREEN INGRAM
ILLUSTRATIONS BY JOSH GREEN

OTHER BOOKS BY DOREEN INGRAM

MY SANCTUARY
THE MISSION
SQUIRRELLY SALLY

Copyright 2017
All rights reserved, Ingram Swanson & Company, LLC.
Second Edition

Interior design by J.K. Eckert & Company, Inc.

All rights reserved. No part of this publication may be reproduced or transmitted in any form or by any means, including photocopying, recording, or other electronic or mechanical methods, without the prior written permission of the publisher, except in the case of brief quotations embodied in critical reviews and certain non-commercial uses permitted by copyright laws.

Ingram Swanson & Company, LLC.
2831 St. Rose Parkway, Suite 450
Henderson, NV 89052

www.myplacecalledhome.com

ISBN: 978-0-9915252-3-2

Contents

Preface v

Chapter 1 – A Life Forever Changed 1

Chapter 2 – Showtime! 8

Chapter 3 – Change of Heart 16

Chapter 4 – A New Day 27

Chapter 5 – One Step Closer to Freedom 34

Chapter 6 – King at Last 43

Photographs 47

Glossary 50

About Jonathan Kraft 53

About the Author 57

Preface

I dedicate this book to Jonathan Kraft's "Keepers of the Wild" and all the good sanctuaries in the world that give everything they have to rescue and follow up with the difficult task of caring for abused, neglected, and homeless animals. It's hard to turn down an animal in need, but sometimes, for the good of all the other ones they have in their care, they must. One way to help is to make sure you never support in any way a business that breeds exotics or uses them in any way to entertain people. I hope, through reading my books, that children and adults will conclude that animals have feelings and a deeper understanding of their world than they are credited with. I've seen it with my own eyes: the love of a mother gorilla who holds her baby so close and rocks it like I did with my babies, staring at them in awe of their beauty and innocence. A lion will sometimes bring food to an injured member of their pride. An elephant family will protect a baby elephant, surrounding it with their own bodies when danger is present. With so many beautiful stories around us of animals taking care of their own and of others, it makes the job of writing stories easy for me.

I believe that sharing lots of facts about animals along with their true stories will encourage empathy in my readers. Don't we need more of that in all societies? As with humans, bad things happen in the lives of animals, too, and though many times it's so sad that we might not want to read on, we do, because we grow and learn and hopefully take with us a better understanding of life around us.

The population of the Big Cats in the wild is dwindling fast, and there are more in captivity in the United States of America than in the wild. All countries are suffering huge declines in their wildlife population because of poor policies and the destructive practices of cutting down, burning, and demolishing everything and anything in sight for human use and consumption. I believe we all can make a change and still live well without destroying the ecosystem that is crucial to support the continued existence of wildlife on our planet.

Thank you, Jonathan Kraft, for seeing that exotic animals should not be used for entertainment and for acting accordingly. The love and energy you put forth for the animals is contagious. You and Tina have laughed and cried through the good times and bad, and still move forward with the energy and love I wish more people had. Exhaustion seems never to win, because you know that out there, somewhere, there is another animal that needs a safe, good home. It needs you to help it to have a place it can and will always call home.

Special thanks to Shara Johnson, of skjtravel.net, for all the editing assistance. To Josh Green, illustrator, and to J. K. Eckert and Company, for typography and page composition.

Chapter 1

A Life Forever Changed

The silence is broken by the clanking of locks and cages being opened. It's that time again: time to perform. I've become accustomed to each performance and usually do it without complaint or hesitation. It's a way to get out of the cage that I'm in most of the day. Today is not one of those usual days, though. My mood is not good. I'm stiff from lying in my cage so many hours, and my stomach doesn't feel well. How do I tell my master how I feel? I can't. All I can do is disobey and not leave the cage when I'm called. Maybe then he'll see that something is wrong.

My name is Elvis, and I am an African lion. I was named after a famous singer and actor who also did a lot of performances in Las Vegas, Nevada, where I now live. Although it was Elvis' decision to perform, it has not been mine.

I'm one of the luckier lions. My master is compassionate, and I have never been hit by him or treated unkindly. Many of the big cats that entertain people aren't so lucky. They're beaten and forced to perform. If they refuse to do so, they may be abused even more. Although my master doesn't understand that I shouldn't be in a cage to entertain people, he isn't a bad person, just ill-informed, like many other people. And speaking of Jonathan, here he comes. He's dressed in a silly, shiny costume that sparkles in the light. He carries a stick with him at all times. They call it a *No No* or *Spook Stick*. It's used on the animals when they're being trained to perform, or if they aren't doing what they're supposed to do. The masters use it for their own protection, too.

He calls me for a second time as he holds the door of the cage open, expecting me to come out. By now I can tell by the sound of his voice that he isn't happy about me not leaving the cage. "Too bad," I think. I continue to lie on the floor of my cage and stare into his eyes. He knows me well; he backs up, closes the cage door and bolts it shut.

"Good! Good," I think, as he walks away in that silly, shiny suit. I got my way today, but I had better be careful and obey tomorrow or things might get bad for me. Oh, I know I could take any man down with one swipe of my huge paw, claws extended. My retractable claws are designed to catch large prey in the wild like wildebeest, zebra, gazelle, wild pigs, and other hoofed animals whose natural habitat happens to be the same place my distant family comes from: Africa. In Africa, the lion is the king of his territory, with only humans and other lions as predators.

There were once millions of lions roaming the savanna, the grassy plains and woodlands of Africa. A few more than 300 lions live in a protected area in the Gir Forest in Asia, but the rest of the remaining wild lions call Africa their home. I have heard that there are more lions in captivity than in the wild now. I'm proof of that!

As my master leaves to fetch another animal to take my place today, I close my eyes, and my mind wanders off to another time in my life—a time of pain, loneliness, helplessness, and terror. I go back to a time when I was a young cub, a time that will be in my memory for the rest of my life. I was only a few months old when I was taken from my mother and my brothers and sisters. There I was alone, with my eyes closed, as the darkness of the room made it useless to keep them open, and I was tired—so very tired. It seemed like forever to me but, just three days earlier, I had been removed from my beloved family. I missed my beautiful mom with her soft fur that was warm and comfortable, and I missed her kisses. Her tongue was rough and, like all lions', she could clean the meat off the bones of her meals with it. But she gently licked her cubs to clean us and give affection. It was also a way of bonding with each other. You see, families are an important part of a lion's life. Wild lions live in prides that consist of one or two males and lots of females and cubs. There is safety in numbers, and it also increases the chance of survival. The females work together as a team to chase down and catch prey to feed the pride.

The males, or dads, of the pride patrol their territory, watch over the cubs while the moms are away hunting for food, and keep the pride safe from other male lions that might try to take over the family.

I felt safe and at peace when I was with my mom. At times, she would lift her chin, wrinkle up her nose, and open her mouth to read someone's scent. She always knew when someone was coming and when it was feeding time. Lions can detect scents from other lions and animals by using these special glands. We also have scent glands on our tails and even between our toes!

But now I was alone and in a dark and lonely place. I could hear noises of other animals crying out for help or moaning with loneliness. I even heard some roars that sounded similar to my mother's, and I knew there were more of my kind in that place. Humans took me out of my small, cold, steel cage long enough to pop a bottle into my mouth. The milk didn't taste like my mother's milk, but I drank because I was hungry. When the lights were turned on in the building, I could see many cages, large and small. A few of the animals inside looked familiar to me, but many did not. They walked on four legs and had fur, but it wasn't like mine. Some of the fur was striped, some had spots. I would find out later that they were tigers and leopards. Some were large, and some were smaller, such as the lynx and bobcats. As I looked around this large warehouse, my eyes came to stop at the large cage located beside mine. There was a male lion with a mane, thick and long and amazing to me. My mother did not have a mane; only a male lion has one, and this was the first time I'd seen one. My mother told me I would also have a mane someday when I was a little older. I couldn't wait.

I looked intently upon this great lion and worked up the courage to squeak out a hello. I was a bit intimidated by his presence but curious just the same.

"Hello," I said, so softly that I couldn't even hear myself. "Hello," I tried again. He opened one of his eyes and then shut it again. I tried a third time, and this time he answered.

"Hello, young one."

"Sir, please, can you tell me where I am? What's this place I've been taken to, and where is my mother?"

"If you must know," he said, his voice deep and low, "it's a place they call an auction house."

"A what house?" I asked with a bit of a shaky voice. This didn't sound good to me.

"An auction house, a place where humans buy and sell animals—in our case, exotic wildlife, big and small cats. You know: lions, tigers, cheetahs, cougars, leopards, and others."

"Okay. And what do they do to us once we're sold?" I was truly afraid to hear his reply, but I had to find out what was to be done to me. I guessed I wouldn't be returning to my family, and my heart felt like it was up in my throat, and I wanted to cry.

"Well, young man, there are lots of things that can be done with you. As for me, I'm being sold to be used for a canned hunt. I'll be released to a large field or farm, and then I will be shot and killed by a hunter who pays money to hunt me down. I'll become a decoration, as humans would say, for a mantelpiece above a fireplace, or a rug, or stuffed and put in a room to be viewed by other humans. So much for the 'King of the Jungle,' ha? King of nothing now! So, please, leave me be and let me sleep. It's all I have now. Good luck to you, son."

I will never forget the look on his massive and handsome face. It was a look of despair and misery. There was no hope for him. I shivered in my cage, unsure if there was any hope for me, either. I would just have to wait and see when it was my turn to be sold.

Chapter 2

SHOWTIME!

I awoke early, as usual, this morning. Yesterday's tummy ache is history, and I feel much better. Memories of my youth have been pushed aside for the time being, and I await my master's arrival. I'm ready to get out of this cage! With all four paws on the floor, I walk in the typical pattern. Walk to the left corner then to the right, back to the left, over and over in my cage. It's my only way of getting exercise. The size of my cage is just about as big as a boxcar on a train, and it's where I eat and sleep. I hear the familiar clinking and clanking sounds as my master peeks around the corner and calls out my name.

"Elvis?" There seems to be a slight questioning tone in his voice. I answer with a low and soft moan—***m–oww, m–oww***—which reassures him that I'm back to normal. The door to my cage is opening, and I leap at him standing on two legs, front legs flung around his shoulders. No, I don't want to eat him. I'm just happy to see him, and I feel well today. I nearly knock him down because I outweigh him by more than 400 pounds! I settle down and lean over the wooden box that I sleep in, and I get a few pets before we leave.

With a click of the chain, he latches my decorative jeweled collar, and away we go to the holding crate that will transfer me and the other animals to the educational arena, called "Predators Paradise," where the shows will be performed.

I'm not alone in the truck, as there are various other animals that are moved to the show along with me. For starters, there is Sampson, also an African lion and newest member of our show. He takes my place when I'm not feeling well, which does happen sometimes. Raja, well, he's a massive Siberian tiger! He's special, all right. All of the tigers are, really. They are a bit different from me and Sampson, because they have stripes on their fur that provide camouflage in the wild. If all of their fur was shaved off, the same stripes and markings could still be seen, because it's also on their skin, and every tiger has a different pattern. That's a unique quality I wouldn't mind having myself! My friend who lives beside my cage is named Natasha. She's a Bengal tiger, and what a beautiful girl she is! She's not my type, though. My type doesn't have stripes or spots. I'm looking for a beauty who can roar like me!

While listening to my masters during the shows, I've learned that, at one time, there were nine different types, or subspecies, of tigers *(Panthera Tigris)* in the wild; now there are only six. Three types of tigers are extinct, and soon more will be gone—gone forever from the place they called home. One of the biggest reasons the tigers and other big cats are disappearing from their homes is because of habitat loss—that is, humans moved onto their land or cut down their forests so they have no place to live and find food. Thousands are hunted down and killed for their fur or to decorate a home or office. Many, like my sad friend from the auction house, are raised to be used for "canned hunts." They never get to roam free or feel the grass underneath their feet until the dreadful day they are released into a field only to be shot down and become someone's trophy.

Last but not least of the big cats in the show is Hope. She's a black jaguar, and her body is built lower to the ground than any of the other big cats. Maybe this is the reason the jaguars are known to be more successful in taking down their prey than lions or tigers. They are the third largest big cat *(Panthera onca)* and kill their prey by using their powerful jaws to bite down on the skull of a mammal or on an armored reptile such as a turtle. That kind of power might scare others, but Hope is a good friend of mine, and we get along just fine. In the wild, she wouldn't want to be my friend, because she is just like the tiger—a solitary animal. That's no fun to me, because I enjoy the company of others.

I hear the words "load 'em up," and we're all ready for the short drive down the road to the arena where the show is held. Once we arrive, another strange-looking vehicle takes all the cages, the animals included, to a covered area behind the arena until it's our turn to **perform**. Hope is first and, as our master, Jonathan, takes her out of her crate, she gives me a wink. She isn't my type, either, but she thinks she is. I guess that's okay. It's not my fault I'm so strikingly attractive! I just lay my head down on my soft furry paw and sleep until I'm called.

It's my turn now, and I'm led out to the arena. It's decorated to look like the Serengeti Plains of Africa. Jonathan's partner introduces me by describing some of the natural habitat in Africa. "This is Elvis," he points to me. Chained with a leash that Jonathan's holding, I jump onto the prop. This rock, or prop, as it's called in "show business," is not real. It's just hard plastic, shaped and painted to look like a real boulder. There are also trees and some shrubbery that are used as props for the show, but they're not real, either.

As Jonathan begins his talk, I just sit upon my fake rock looking ever so handsome. "This is Elvis, and he's an African lion and one of the four big cats in the genus **Panthera**. He is a **Panthera leo**." Jonathan talks through an object called a microphone; the audience is able to hear the excitement in his voice, and they listen intently. Well, that is until one of the children decides to be naughty and begins to whine that he is standing too long! While we wait for the child to quiet down, I lift my lip, open my mouth, and catch the smell of popcorn! My mouth begins to salivate, and I find myself drooling. I sometimes enjoy the taste of the popcorn people leave behind, picking it up with my mouth as I'm led out of the staged area. Although I'm a carnivore—strictly a meat eater—I enjoy an occasional snack!

One of the people in the audience has asked a question.

"Who is the largest of the big cats?"

"The tiger is," my master Jonathan answers, "and specifically the Siberian tiger." I can just imagine Raja and Natasha now, looking proud to be the largest breed of big cats. Well, that's fine with me, but I believe lions have more fun! Jonathan tells the audience that lions are the second largest of the big cats, followed by the jaguar and then leopard.

My part of the show is almost over, and I end it with my famous **roar**. Beginning with some short rumbles, I end with a deep and loud **R–A–W–RRR!** It always gets attention—sometimes almost five miles down the road! Yes, a lion's roar can be heard a long way away. One last question rises from the audience. I turn to Jonathan, and he gestures for me to stay. I do as I'm told. A child asks a question I have heard many times while I'm on stage. "Why doesn't Elvis have a mane? Don't all male lions have manes?"

"Great question," I hear my master reply. "Elvis is a little different from other male lions. Like many lions used for entertainment or sold as pets, he was born from a lioness that was kept alive only so she would produce babies, which are called **cubs.** Her cubs were then auctioned off to the highest bidder, that is to say, sold to the person who offered the most money. Elvis was sold, when he was only a few months old, to a woman who wanted to use him in a dancing show. She purchased him from an auction house."

Oh, that word! My hair stands up on my back just thinking about it!

"She was going to train Elvis to do tricks for the show. He was taken to a place in Nevada that was home to an exotic animal trainer whose methods were terrifying. This trainer believed that letting Elvis be attacked by vicious dogs would scare him so badly that he would obey his owner and, in turn, be easily taught to do whatever the trainer wanted him to do. Elvis was very young and too small to defend himself. The dogs mauled him and inflicted many bite wounds. Fortunately, before he was permanently scarred, some good people came to Elvis's rescue. Frightened and weak, he was rescued and taken to a place that provides shelter for unwanted animals. But he had to live in a cage all alone, secluded from every other animal. Because he was growing bigger, and likely more dangerous every day, the people at the shelter decided to perform a special type of operation on him and hoped it would help prevent him from getting too wild to handle. A veterinarian did the surgery. It not only made it impossible for Elvis to become a dad one day, but also prevented him from growing a mane like other male lions have. As a result, his head and body grew extra large, and he may have more physical problems."

Now that Jonathan is finished speaking, everyone's looking at me with sad eyes, and I just want to get out of here. This kind of stuff always brings back memories that I would much prefer to forget. I guess that's life, though, and it seems I don't have a choice in the matter. Finally, Jonathan leads me off the African stage and back into my crate. He strokes my head over and over and gives me a kiss right on the mouth! It's okay; I don't mind human germs. It's very comforting, and I love my master. But I'm not happy! Three shows every day, six days a week—sitting, sitting, waiting, and waiting… Maybe tomorrow there will be a change in my life.

Tomorrow, tomorrow, there's always tomorrow.

Chapter 3

Change of Heart

Hope, the black jaguar, begins to moan loudly when she hears our masters' voices. Both men are walking down the dirt path beside our sleeping quarters. I, too, sit straight up in my cage and give them a quiet **m-oww** as they arrive. With leashes in hand, Jonathan takes Hope out of her enclosure, and David gets Sampson. They're led away to the small dirt field where the men pause to discuss the day's events. The two cats use the time to visit with each other.

I can hear Hope asking Sampson about his life before he was brought here. Sampson is one of the newer cats in the show, and I'm also interested in hearing

about his past life. Is it at all like mine? Sampson has now sat down thoughtfully. He seems to be looking off in the distance as if he can see his past life somewhere beyond the field. The sunlight shines on his burnt-orange-colored fur, and his mane is long and full. Eventually, Hope lies down near his feet with her head on her paws, listening.

"I lived the life of a circus cat. Those were tough days…traveling long distances from place to place, stuffed in small train compartments for days at a time. No life for a lion, for sure! Sometimes the heat and stagnant air were almost unbearable, and I felt I could not breathe! There was no way to stay clean, since we were not allowed to leave the compartment on the train until the circus tent was all set up. We slept, ate, and went to the bathroom in that small space. Once the circus crew had everything prepared, we were moved but continued to be confined to our small cages. For all the big cats in the circus act, it was agony; the applause during shows was deafening, and show schedules were exhausting.

"The poor elephants fared even worse, as they were chained by one leg close to a heavy pole or log. Bernice was one of the five huge elephants, or *pachyderms* (which means "thick-skinned"), and though she had been with the circus for more than fifteen years, her heart still mourned for her family back home in India where she was born. She shared her experiences with the circus animals, because many of us had no idea what living in the **wild** was like, and we were always interested in the stories she told. In some ways, an elephant herd is much like a lion's pride, as

they both have close family bonds. The babies are guarded with diligence by each family member, which includes the oldest mother (or "matriarch"), sisters, aunts, and cousins. Bernice told me how her family would walk for miles and miles every day and knew the path so well because it had been used by many generations of elephants. The matriarch was the leader of the herd, and she was the wisest of all the family members. The others trusted her and always followed her. Bernice had happy memories of when the family spent time at the watering holes. That was so much fun for her. The babies enjoyed playing in the water and spraying it over their bodies. Their magnificent long trunks are more than a nose that can smell. They are used to suck up water, grab hold of and bring food to their mouths, move things, and even dig. They even use their trunks to greet each other. They are not carnivores like we are, Hope; they're herbivores and only eat vegetation—leaves, grasses, and that sort of thing.

"Anyway, as time went by, Bernice began to get infections in her feet, and she was in pain every day of her life. But that didn't matter to the circus owner. He made her continue the rigorous daily routines, which meant standing on two feet for long periods of time and doing tricks. The men would hit the elephants with a bull hook to manage them, and many times I watched while they were hit so hard with it that blood leaked from their skin.

Eventually, Bernice gave up hope, and one morning I awoke to see her being hauled away on a trailer. She had died in the night. That was one of the saddest days of my life. But now she is free. Bernice can't be tortured any longer. The circus owner didn't even mourn her death; he had already been training another young elephant to take her place. It was shameful, Hope, utterly shameful.

"As for the big cats, we were trained and forced to perform demeaning and unnatural tricks to entertain the public. Many times we were whipped when we didn't follow the routine our masters planned for us. Once I was hit on my back with a whip so hard I could feel it burn my flesh. It hurt terribly, and I cried in pain. I cowered in a corner, hoping my master would see that I was sorry for making a mistake. I licked my wound, and eventually my flesh healed, but my spirit felt broken. That's exactly what the trainers wanted to happen to us; they thought our broken spirits would cause us to obey them and do the shows properly.

"Some of the tigers in the show had been used for photo opportunities when they were young. People paid money to have their picture taken with a tiger. The tigers were chained tightly and handed from one paying customer to the next. When a tiger cub weighed around eighty pounds, or turned six months old, it was sold at an auction or to another circus or roadside show because, at that weight, the animal could be dangerous enough to hurt a customer—even kill someone! As for me, I was sold as a young cub to this circus and was trained to entertain. I had to jump through a burning hoop, and though I didn't like fire, I feared the whip more. People found that trick wonderful; I found it humiliating and degrading. Jump through hoops, follow the leader, stand on two legs, and prance around!"

"It was terrible," Sampson says sadly. "Just terrible."

I watch Sampson lie down as if he's exhausted, and I feel exhausted, too, listening to what he and Bernice and the others in his past life endured. I wish I could be near Sampson now and rub my head against his to show him some affection. But I'm stuck in this small enclosure.

"So, Hope, what's your story?" Sampson asks, looking up at the sky now, on his back. "Were you part of a circus act before you came here?"

"Oh, no, no, I was a pet!" Hope says and sits up straight. She licks a front paw and inspects it; it looks clean to me.

"How can a big jaguar be a pet?"

I'm wondering the same thing as Sampson. How could a big cat be someone's pet? Hmm. With my ears perked and pressed against the cage bars, I strain to hear the details.

21

"I had a home, for a while at least. A human family bought me from a breeder, so I was taken away from my mother when I was only a few weeks old. Don't ask me anything about my family, because I can't remember. But as I grew older, I was allowed to roam free at a large ranch. People came and went; seldom was I chained. I was fed well, and sometimes I stalked and caught my own prey. There were rabbits and other small animals that would enter the large fenced ranch, and they became my dinner.

"I now believe that I was a **guard** for the property, as it would be a very bad idea for a stranger to climb over the fence or dig underneath it when a jaguar is about! My owners also enjoyed having an exotic animal to show off to visitors. Then I was taken away and brought here. Word is, my owners might have been drug dealers and were put in jail. I didn't do anything wrong, and yet I feel I've now been put in jail, too, since I'm unable to roam freely about the ranch where I once lived. You know, Sampson, I'd rather be killed living out a wild life than die of old age living out someone else's dream."

We're all quiet and somber now, while our masters continue to chat. Though I know the love they have for all the animals here, they have no idea what sad stories have just been told. I sit at the corner and edge of my small enclosure, looking out at the traveling crates lined up and ready to be loaded on the trailer. None of these animals is living a natural life, and it's sad to me. Other animals, besides the big cats, are included in the shows each day. There is an ostrich, a llama, a donkey, and a wolf, and they each have a small enclosure of their own. The only real predator and carnivore in that bunch is the wolf. The other animals are herbivores and a predator's prey. In other words, in the wild, they would all be food for a big cat.

It's time to get loaded up for the short trip to the arena, and then it's showtime. Once the vehicle has stopped and cages are removed from the truck, we have to wait our turn to perform. While we wait, there's nothing much to do but sleep, which naturally I love doing, anyway. I'm retrieved by my master and, as usual, I'm ready to go! The chain is hooked to my collar as we walk a short distance to the exhibition area. I jump on the plastic rock that lies in the middle of the stage and yawn widely, showing off my huge, sharp, white canines. As I shut my mouth, my eyes catch sight of a brightly colored headpiece placed at a slightly crooked angle on the head of a lady. The hat is the color of blood. It has no scent of meat, but I can feel my mouth begin to salivate—the thought of food is regularly on my mind. The sight of red makes me hungry. In the wild, if a lion isn't sleeping or lounging about, he's eating! Big cats are predators, as you know.

Something else keeps my attention on this lady with the blood-red hat. Instead of moving on to the next show, she stays at our "African Safari" exhibit long after the other people leave. My master begins to chat with her, and she's telling him something about keeping big cats for use in show business. I hear him call her Stephanie, and the look on her face is very serious. "Jonathan," she spoke. "When will people quit using these beautiful wild creatures for amusement and entertainment? We both believe they deserve a better life, and since you already rescue animals and are working on teaching others about their plight, why don't you just open your own sanctuary and give them a place they can call home?"

My master is silent, I would say thoughtful. He looks at the floor, deep in thought. I pull at my chain, not knowing what I'm supposed to do now. Usually, Jonathan walks me right back to my holding crate, but he is still standing in the same spot.

Eventually, Stephanie moves on, and I'm taken back to my crate until the next show, which will be two hours from now. Something unusual has happened today. I can sense something changing in Jonathan's heart. He's left me now and gone on to get the next animal for the show.

"Hi, Elvis, how was the show today? Get any popcorn?" Natasha asked me.

"No. But there was something very different about today."

"And what was that, Elvis?"

"There was a special person in the audience today. It was a lady with a big red hat, and she spoke to our master for some time after the show. I noticed an emotion well up in him that I haven't seen before."

"Well, I hope he feels better tomorrow," Natasha says.

"I do, too!" Hope adds.

"Well, we have two more shows to go today, so we'll see," I say.

§ § § § §

The days have continued to be the same as always: short walk to the holding crates, ride to the arena, and sit. Do three shows, back to the crates, load into the trailer, ride back to the enclosure and into the night rooms, eat, and sleep.

Until this morning. Rather than going to do the show, we're being taken to a new place. The drive is much longer than I'm used to. The transport truck is coming to a stop, but there is an unusual silence. There are no crowds of people, only two other vehicles and some buildings along with many medium-sized, fenced outdoor enclosures. There's a lady waiting here, and she claps her hands in delight when our master opens the door of the truck and gets out. They greet each other with a hug, and though I've seen her before at some of the shows, I feel I may be seeing much more of her from now on. It's just instinct, but I feel a bond between her and my master.

Her name is Tina, and I'm happy for her to take part in our care. She looks very friendly, and being pretty doesn't hurt much, either! The sun is slowly setting now, and all of us animals are in new enclosures. Mine is pretty nice; I have more room to walk around. I'm looking forward to what tomorrow brings, but for now, it's time to sleep.

Chapter 4

A New Day

It's as if my life has started over again. I find peace in my day-to-day existence. The other animals and I are so happy to lie around in our new enclosures without the hectic and stressful show schedule we've become accustomed to. Each day, we look forward to being released into a designated fenced area where each of us is allowed a few hours of play and leisure time. Even though the earth beneath my feet is rocky and hard, it's quite different from the cement floors in cages that many big cats call home. It just feels good and natural underneath my paws. My favorite spot in this area is in the shade of a large cottonwood  tree where I relax after having some fun romping around with Jonathan or Tina. I also get a better view of my surroundings and enjoy watching the activity around me. The entertainment world has taken a toll on my body, but my soul is more at peace than ever before. I seldom think about my past anymore. There is no point in dwelling on the bad things, so I do the best I can to enjoy the moments when I get to play with my friends and a new girl named Sheena. She roars like me, looks like me, and smells like me. She's just a lot smaller. I feel myself getting goose bumps just thinking about her. Do lions get goose bumps?

Speaking of friends, Tina isn't here this morning. I wonder if she's gone to fetch another animal who is in need of help. Jonathan calls this place a "sanctuary," and it's a home for "retired exotic wildlife." Retired? I guess that's what all of us are considered now—retired from the entertainment world. Since a male lion usually lives to a little more than fourteen years of age, I'm glad the time I have left will be peaceful, as I am already seven years old.

Did I say "peaceful"? Guess I spoke too soon, because the truck has just pulled into the driveway. Tina's driving, and there are several cages in the back. There's so much noise and commotion that I begin to pace in my cage. What could make such a screeching sound as this?

Monkeys! Oh, I've heard about these primates from some of my other show friends but have never seen one with my own eyes. They are quite unique! Tina says to the other people gathered around, "Well, let's welcome home our new friends. These are the primates that Sheriff Joseph Arpaio rescued! All safe and sound, so let's get to work everyone!"

The monkeys are all different from one another and are of various species of primates. Some have long tails, a few have no tails, and there is even an animal called a **ring-tailed lemur** that has a very long, black-and-white striped tail. I'm amazed at the sight but also very irritated that my peaceful day has been ruined. I continue to watch as, one by one, the crates of monkeys are unloaded from the truck bed by all the keepers and volunteers. I see a very large monkey that's reminding me of a story told by a leopard that had once lived in Africa. He had been captured and brought to America as a cub. He was the only big cat I'd ever met who was actually born in his native country. He passed away several years ago, but I can recall the stories clearly and, if they are true, this is almost certainly a baboon!

Some of the monkeys get to stay together in one cage, but the lemur with the black-and-white striped tail gets a room of his—or I should say her—own. Then there's that baboon. He doesn't look happy and makes some very intimidating gestures with his mouth, showing his very large canines. These teeth can grow to about two inches long, which is about the same size as mine, and are sometimes referred to as **fangs.** Of course, he doesn't frighten me, since I'm at the top of the food chain, but I feel a bit uneasy with the way he jumps at the cage and quickly runs from side to side. He seems to like picking up handfuls of sand and rock and throwing them at any human who comes close to his cage. I hope he'll fall asleep soon, because he's making me nervous. I'll sleep better when he has quieted down.

§ § § § §

It's a new day, and the sun has begun to rise. All the animals are being pulled awake by its light. The baboon's covered enclosure is across the pathway from mine, and I'm curious to know what his name is.

"My name's Billy, and I'm an *olive baboon,* for your information," he replies when I ask.

"Billy, that's a nice name. I was just wondering where you came from; why are you here?"

"Long story," he says as he sits down and grasps the bars of his cage with his human-like hands— four fingers and a thumb, just like Jonathan. "Let's just say I got out of hand. Chained to a bed rail, I broke loose and sort of tore my owner's apartment to shreds. I just couldn't stand it anymore and had to get away! My punishment was to be sent away. I'm dangerous and unpredictable. Well, no kidding, I'm a wild animal! When has that become news?"

Billy is staring at the ground now. He looks so sad—no longer angry, only very sad. He's been taken away from the only family he's ever known and now has no idea what his life will be like. He seems to have loved his master, as I did and still do, but as most stories go that start with humans having wildlife as pets, it ended terribly for Billy. Such stories seldom have happy endings.

Alone in his new enclosure, he moves off to the corner and lays his head on the ground. I can see him shaking, and I feel very sorry for this creature. But I have no words at this time to console him. It's hard enough for me to grasp all the changes that have taken place lately; I can hardly help him to understand also. I shut my eyes as well and look forward to playtime with Sheena, Natasha, and Hope. It occurs to me that there's a special meaning behind the name of my friend: Hope. I wish I could tell Billy that there is hope for a better future. He should never give up, or he might miss his chance at happiness. I don't know if he can understand this, but when he wakes up, I'll do my best to make him feel better.

§ § § § § §

The other animals from the show seem quite at home with our new life. The donkey is allowed to roam about freely during the day, and he enjoys picking and eating at grasses, leaves, and small bushes. There aren't a lot of large plants here, as we live in a desert environment, but there is enough to munch on and stay busy throughout the day.

The gray wolf, Montana, whom Jonathan had used in the educational wildlife theme park along with the rest of us, is now joined by several other young wolves that have been rescued and brought to our sanctuary. Because of his age, size, and strength, I'm sure he'll be the wolf in charge or, as they say, the **"alpha."** Good for you, Montana! Finally, this dark-furred wolf can live a more natural life, because it's not in a wolf's nature to live alone. Like the lions, in the wild, wolves rely on the whole group to find food and keep the pack safe and growing. When the sun disappears each night, they begin to howl, and it sounds almost like a song—each wolf is in tune with the other members of the pack. Hope says she finds it quite lovely. I must agree, but it's very loud indeed.

It's been a long and slightly chaotic week, but I can't wait to see what another day brings.

Chapter 5

One Step Closer to Freedom

"Start an intravenous drip, stat!"

Though I'm weary and feel sleepy, I can still hear Dr. Erika Koenig, the veterinarian, calling out orders to the animal technicians. I don't know how I got here, but I'm lying on a table, surrounded by Jonathan, Tina, and other people I don't know. I feel like I'm drowning. It's hard to breathe.

Now someone has put a mask over my face, and oxygen is flowing. Ah, that's better. It's easier to breathe now. Something has gone wrong with my kidneys, and I'm very sick. I can't remember the last time I felt like eating. Imagine a lion losing his appetite! Lately, I've been thirsty all the time, and I haven't felt like my jolly self for a while now. Luckily, Jonathan noticed I wasn't feeling right. Dr. Koenig says I'm in renal failure. Just when life is getting better…leave it to me to get sick.

Thank goodness, though, I was helped before it was too late. With the good care of the doctor and her staff, I only had to spend a few weeks in the hospital, and now I'm ready to go home. Yay! I can't wait to see Sheena and the rest of my friends, and I've missed our romping and playtimes. I wonder how Billy the baboon is doing. Here comes Jonathan with the big truck to pick me up. I'm ready and willing to obey his commands and to get in the travel crate, because I know I'm **going home.**

The drive seems extra long back to our home. Maybe it's just because I have been kind of out of it for a while now.

"We're here!" Jonathan is yelling out the open window in the cab of the truck. Here? Where's here? This isn't my home. What happened to my home? I don't understand what's going on. Where are my friends? I feel panicked. Where's Billy the baboon and those irritating monkeys? I'm snarling now, looking through the bars of my travel crate, because I'm very upset.

As we drive down a short dirt road, we pass a small, reddish brown building on one side and a tan and brown one on the opposite side of the road. We drive very slowly and, from the truck, I can see Sampson in a large, natural-looking habitat. He isn't restricted to a small enclosure anymore, and neither are my other friends. Never in my life have I known that kind of freedom! Our wooden sleeping boxes are inside the enclosures, but the amount of space shared by each animal group in their habitats is amazing. We stop, and Jonathan gets out of the truck. Tina and the keepers are now helping to move my crate onto a trailer that is hooked onto a small vehicle that Jonathan is now driving. The team walks beside us as we drive a short way and stop near a fenced habitat. There are my good friends, Hope and Natasha! Oh, it's so good to see them, and it is enough to calm my nerves. I let out a big happy rumble and **r–aow** to let them know I'm okay.

"This is your new home, Elvis!" Tina exclaims. She seems quite happy, and this puts any fears I have left to rest. My crate is being moved into a new habitat

where I'm now being released. It's right next door to Hope's. My biggest surprise is that the beautiful Sheena and I are sharing one habitat. Now I know I'm in heaven!

"Hello, my friend!" she exclaimed.

"What is this, Sheena? What's this all about?"

"Home," she said. "Welcome, my dear friend, to your new home."

§ § § § § §

Everyone has gone back to doing the daily chores, and I have a chance now to look around a bit. One paw at a time, I step out into the rocky desert habitat. I keep walking straight ahead—another step—okay, one more. Wow! I take more and more steps. I can't believe it! I'm running! Hey, what's that thing with the fuzzy long tail? It looks like fun; I think I'll chase it. Yes, I'm running and chasing it! What fun this is!

Oh, what is this new life? Suddenly, I have a newfound freedom I've only ever dreamed about. Not sure what to do next, but I think I'll join Sheena on the boulder over there. Yes, I'll jump on it and sit for as long as I want! I wish I could ask Jonathan if I can stay here in this wonderful piece of freedom. Though Sheena has already told me I can, I still need the reassurance of Jonathan. I no longer think of him as my master—just a good and loving "friend."

I join Sheena on a large, pale, red-and-tan-colored boulder. She scoots over a bit to give me some space. "Hey, I see you spotted the local squirrels, Elvis. Lots of fun chasing those guys, but they're very fast indeed. Lots of rabbits around, too, and they're not an easy catch, either!"

"Yeah, it was fun…though I can tell I haven't quite regained my strength yet. But, Sheena, I can promise this: if I'm allowed to stay here, I will get better! This is the best day of my life!"

§ § § § §

I can see Billy far away in his new habitat, and he seems happy and at peace. He has a very large ball to play with, climbing ropes, and plenty of things going on around him to keep him occupied. I'm sending Billy a message using my various vocal sounds to let him know that I'm okay. He's heard my **r–aow r–aow r–aow,** and now he's returning the call with lots of quick and loud grunts. His excitement is contagious and arouses the attention of the coyote pair, Jack and Jill. A coyote is similar to a dog, but they're wild and live in small groups. In the fall and winter, they form packs for effective hunting. They're omnivores, which means they can eat everything, both plant and animal life. Though it's normal for coyotes to begin the loud and high-pitched

yipping calls at night, Billy is sure getting a chorus going between them and the exotic birds that were rescued and now live in a large enclosure down the dirt road. It's quite noisy!

There's a young lion cub here named Anthony, who was confiscated, or taken away, from a lady who was trying to sell him for money. He is in very good shape right now but has a very bad sore on his little face. It's called "cage rub," and it's caused by being in a small cage for too long. A baby coyote named Riley has recently arrived at the sanctuary, as well, and he was all alone. Normally, the coyote pups stay with their mom and dad for around two years, then move on to find a mate of their own, but this little girl was abandoned for some reason. She was brought in by the Fish and Game wildlife agency. Anthony and the coyote are sharing an enclosure, at least for the time being, because they're both babies, and they need a friend so they won't be so lonely and scared. It's quite odd to see the coyote, Riley, and the lion cub playing together in their enclosure. Hope tells me they even sleep together. She says that, of all things, at feeding time, Riley sometimes takes the food right out of Anthony's mouth! I haven't quite figured this out yet, but maybe it doesn't matter whether they are of the same species. I think they both just needed a friend and a warm pal to snuggle up with. Maybe it takes some of the pain out of being separated from their families.

   I can already sense that this will be the last move I'll ever make. I wish I could share this news with others so they, too, could have some hope of a better life. I can only tell my story as I've lived it, and maybe one day it can make a difference to all the animals that are used for entertainment purposes. As for all of the orphans here at this sanctuary, I believe I speak for them to say we are all content and happy. Most of us will never be able to be released into the wild, as for sure we would perish; we had no parents to teach us how to survive in our natural habitat. But at least we have our dignity.

Now it's nap time for me again. I'm going to lie on my back and open my legs wide to get some sun on my belly. I really enjoy this position, and I'm getting used to the relaxed feel of our beautiful sanctuary home.

Chapter 6

KING AT LAST

The low rumble of another train passes by as the sun peeks around the mountainside, and I awaken to a new day. The crisp, cool wind blows my long whiskers, and it almost tickles. The inhabitants at our sanctuary now include another lion named Sultan, several leopards, and some cougars. Two of the cougars, Baby and Bam Bam, live together in one habitat. Next to them, in a separate area, is Bandit. He was just a cub when he was given as a gift to an eight-year-old girl. As Bandit got older, bigger, and of course dangerous, the little

girl's mother had the good sense to find a more appropriate home for him. My habitat is located across and down the narrow road from the three cougars, and since I'm king of this sanctuary, I keep a watch on their activity. When I hear a–ow, a–ow, a–ow, I know Jonathan is near, because he is their favorite human.

Similar to the four species of big cats from the **Panthera** genus, the cougar (also called *mountain lion, puma, panther,* or *catamount*) is from the **Felidae** genus and is

the largest of the small cats. Cougars are most closely related to the domestic cat and even have many of the same vocal sounds such as growls, hisses, purrs, and screams. But they cannot roar like the big cats can—not like I can. Nobody can roar like I can! But I do wonder what it feels like to purr, for lions cannot purr. Cougars are silvery gray or reddish colored and have amazing light-and-dark color patterns on their faces, giving them their distinctive look. Though they can adapt well in many environments, the native rocky terrain here at the sanctuary is perfect for them.

Feeding time around here is very interesting! Bam Bam the cougar is screaming for his food, Billy the baboon is grunting loudly, the coyotes are barking and howling, the goats are **maaa**–ing, Natasha is roaring, and I'm just sittin' on my boulder waiting patiently for my fifteen pounds of red, grade-A beef! Some of the tigers have been given their meals, and the crunching, growling, and snarling I hear has made my stomach begin to growl. I can wait no longer! I'm high-tailing it to the front of the habitat to rub against the steel fence, hoping the food cart gets here quickly. Sheena has taken her time, but now she's by my side, also waiting.

"Here comes dinner, Sheena!" I'm heading to my food bowl. **"Grrr–r–aow."**

A loud howl has suddenly come from the wolves' habitat! I see running and hear the sound of walkie-talkies echoing in several areas of the park. I can't tell what's going on! I'm standing on my two back legs and have placed my front paws on the fence to get a better look. When standing, I'm almost ten feet tall, so it makes it easier to check out the situation. Here comes the battery-operated cart, rushing down the road, and all I can see right now is the dust that lingers in the air.

The dust is starting to clear, and I can see some of the keepers, Jonathan, and Tina. Uh-oh. Doesn't look good. One of the wolves has hurt his leg badly, possibly from a fight with one of the other pack members. It's Cheyenne, and I can see he's in pain. Fast as lightning, the keepers are already luring the rest of the wolf clan into the night areas and locking them inside. Now the habitat is empty except for Cheyenne, and the keepers are running toward him, taking care not to fall into one of the deep den holes that the wolf pack has dug into the hard, rocky ground. Two keepers are moving the steel travel crate into the habitat and lifting Cheyenne inside. Off they go now to the animal hospital for treatment. Oh, I hope he'll be okay. I guess it's just part of sanctuary life—never a dull moment.

§ § § § §

Each and every animal here has a story to tell, and many come to this sanctuary with lots of problems from their past abuse and neglect. Speaking of problems, Sheena had a stroke a couple of months ago, and though she still gets around pretty good on her own, I sometimes follow her when she's not having a good day. When I notice her getting a bit wobbly, I walk beside her and keep her steady so she can get to her food and water. It's just what a good partner does—just as a pride of lions would do to help each other survive in the wild, and just as you would do to help your friends when they are in need.

All the animals here have found a good place to live out the rest of their lives, and I'm so thankful that I'm one of them. Although it's not like living in the wild, it comes in close second and is the best it can be. This is a place we **all** call **home.**

ELVIS AND SHEENA

*All photographs courtesy of Tina Matejek. Tina is a lifelong animal lover. Her motivation comes from the love and energy that these beautiful and highly sensitive creatures bestow upon her. Their unique personalities are embraced by her, and it shows as she helps care for these orphaned and abused animals that call "Keepers of the Wild" their final home.

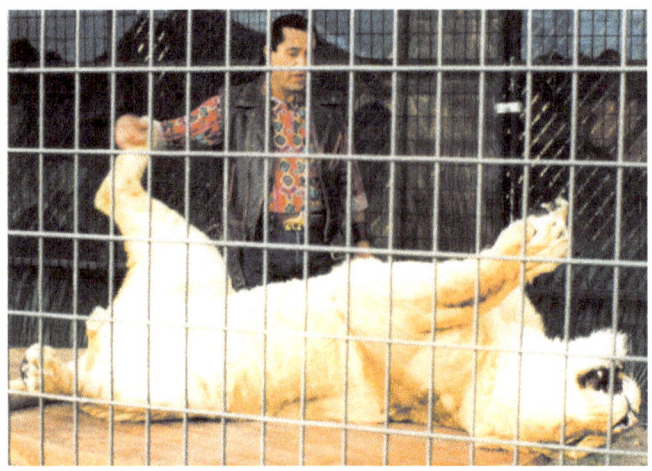 

ELVIS AND JONATHAN

ANTHONY, THE LION CUB
RILEY, THE COYOTE

TINA, DOREEN, AND JONATHAN

TOP: JONATHAN, TINA, AND ALADDIN, A RETIRED ENTERTAINMENT TIGER. BELOW: DEDICATED TO SAMPSON THE TIGER. HE WAS FORTUNATE TO EXPERIENCE HIS LAST SIX MONTHS AT KEEPERS OF THE WILD.

Glossary

Animal abuse: the crime of inflicting physical pain, suffering, or death on an animal, usually a tame one, beyond necessity for normal discipline. It can include neglect that is so monstrous (withholding food and water) that the animal has suffered, died, or been put in imminent danger of death.

Animal instinct: the inherent disposition of a living organism toward a particular behavior.

Big cats: any of several large cats typically able to roar and living in the wild. One definition of "big cat" includes the four members of the genus Panthera: the tiger, lion, jaguar, and leopard. Members of this genus are the only cats able to roar. A more expansive definition of "big cat" also includes the cougar, cheetah, snow leopard, and clouded leopard.

Carnivore: meaning *meat eater*; an organism that derives its energy and nutrient requirements from a diet consisting mainly or exclusively of animal tissue, whether through predation or scavenging. A carnivore that sits at the top of the food chain is an *apex predator*.

Conservation movement: known as *nature conservation;* a political, environmental, and social movement that seeks to protect natural resources including animal, fungus, and plant species as well as their habitat for the future.

Endangered species: a population of organisms facing a high risk of becoming extinct because it is either few in numbers or threatened by changing environmental or predation parameters.

Habitat destruction: the process in which natural habitat is rendered functionally unable to support the species present. In this process, the organisms that previously used the site are displaced or destroyed, reducing biodiversity. Habitat destruction by human activity is mainly for the purpose of harvesting natural resources for industry production and urbanization. Clearing habitats for agriculture is the principal cause of habitat destruction. Other important causes of habitat destruction include mining, logging, trawling, and urban sprawl. Habitat destruction is currently ranked as the primary cause of species extinction worldwide.

Herbivore: an organism that is anatomically and physiologically adapted to eat plant-based foods.

Natural habitat: A *habitat* is an ecological or environmental area that is inhabited by a particular species of animal, plant, or other type of organism. It is the natural environment in which an organism lives, or the physical environment that surrounds (influences and is utilized by) a species population.

Predator: in ecology, *predation* describes a biological interaction where a predator (an organism that is hunting) feeds on its prey (the organism that is attacked). Predators may or may not kill their prey prior to feeding on them, but the act of predation often results in the death of its prey and the eventual absorption of the prey's tissue through consumption.

Omnivore: consumes both animal and non-animal food. Apart from the more general definition, there is no clearly defined ratio of plant to animal material that would distinguish a facultative carnivore from an omnivore, or an omnivore from a facultative herbivore, for that matter.

About Jonathan Kraft

Jonathan Kraft is an animal behaviorist who has a passion for animals that stems from his early childhood. Jonathan left his small hometown in Holland to immigrate to the United States via Canada in pursuit of the "American Dream." He settled and ran a highly successful chain of ballroom dancing studios for more than twenty-two years. Throughout the years, he was exposed to the entertainment industry and soon set his sights on a career in show business.

After establishing himself as a producer, creator, and performer in Las Vegas, Jonathan began working on a multimillion dollar production on the Las Vegas Strip. The show Jonathan was working on stayed in preproduction for three years while he presided over choreographers, showgirls, musicians, set designers, and a small menagerie of exotic animals.

Jonathan's activism in animal issues got started soon after he decided to acquire and train two tiger cubs for his production. While learning to care for his cubs, he was exposed to other animal trainers and witnessed the neglect and abuse that many animal performers suffer behind the scenes. He started to rescue animals while continuing his work with wild animals in movies, TV shows, commercials, documentaries, specials, and a variety of shoots and exhibits.

As Jonathan's reputation for saving animals spread, he started to receive calls from local performers wanting to unload their animals that were unwilling or unable to perform. Jonathan learned that once these magnificent creatures lose their value as performers, they are commonly disposed of. After encountering some of the most heart-wrenching cases of neglect, abuse, and malicious cruelty, he was compelled to take action. Consumed with the full-time care needs of the animals he acquired, he put his production on hiatus.

Being a firm believer in the power of education, he launched his campaign through Predator's Paradise, an educational wildlife theme park at the Aladdin Hotel on the Las Vegas Strip. Though Predator's Paradise was an absolute success, Jonathan came to a full realization that animals in entertainment do not have quality of life, even under the best circumstances. Actress Stephanie Powers frequented his educational shows, and they became acquainted and discovered that they shared a passion for animal welfare and conservation. Powers encouraged Jonathan to look into starting up a sanctuary of his own. Determined to provide his rescued animals with the best quality of life possible, he proceeded to open the much larger Keepers of the Wild.

KEEPERS OF THE WILD NATURE PARK
13441 EAST HIGHWAY 66
VALENTINE, ARIZONA 86437
(928) 769-1800
WWW.KEEPERSOFTHEWILD.ORG

Mission

Keepers of the Wild is a 501(c)(3) nonprofit sanctuary dedicated to the dignified rescue of exotic animals. Internationally recognized, it is our goal to build a facility that will be the standard for all future animal parks…with educational and research facilities that span all ages and diverse programs that offer our visitors artistic and cultural experiences indicative of the countries that our animals come from. We will keep to the high "no breeding" standards that we started with and strive to make the public aware of the challenges faced by some of the world's most exotic and beautiful animals.

—Jonathan Kraft, Founder and Director

SHARA, DOREEN, NICOLE, AND TINA

About the Author

If it weren't for my father, Dale Claiborne, and my mother, Ouida Alderman, who many times allowed me to bring home stray cats and dogs, frogs, lizards, birds, and anything else that was hurt or that I found in need of care, I might not have found myself writing about my most favorite thing in the world besides my three children—animals. Thanks to John Ingram, who has spent many hours helping me make rehabilitation enclosures for the animals I foster for The Wildlife Sanctuary of Northwest Florida and for preparing the videos I use in my school presentations.

Next time you think, "What can I do to help?" remember—one person can make a huge difference. Whether it's donating money or food for a sanctuary or society that's nearest and dearest to your heart, or whether it's donating your time—you can make a difference for the good of many. Never give up!

My thanks go to everyone at Keepers of the Wild sanctuary for all the help with facts and the support you've given to me! Special thanks to Jonathan Kraft, Tina Matejek, Nicole Walls, animal keepers, and volunteers. You all do an excellent job taking care of these animal victims. Bless you all.

www.ingramcontent.com/pod-product-compliance
Lightning Source LLC
Chambersburg PA
CBHW061930290426
44113CB00024B/2869